NEWBURGH THEOLOGICAL SEMINARY

NEWBURGH
COLLEGE OF THE BIBLE

ISBN: 1-59268-750-4

Newburgh Theological Seminary/Newburgh College of the Bible

Newburgh Seminary Press
Newburgh, Indiana

NewburghSeminary@aol.com
Telephone (812) 858-3920
Website www.newburghseminary.com

Cover By: Cecilia Brendel
Manuscript Assistant: John Beanblossom

Printed in the United States of America

Table of Contents

Our President's Welcome

Welcome to Newburgh Theological Seminary! Our school is Christ-centered! The Bible is the greatest book of all! We are here to help you in your journey of a Christ-filled education as you study the greatest book ever written – God's Holy Word! Our school was organized by Helpers In Ministries founded in 1988 for the purpose of reaching the world with the good news of Jesus Christ. The mission of HIM is "doing" and "telling" the good news of Christ. The organization decided years ago that if the gospel is to be told and demonstrated to a lost and hurting world that those who have been called by God to serve Him should be trained and equipped with the very best tools possible to effectively accomplish the work of our Lord and Savior Jesus Christ. This is why Newburgh Theological Seminary was founded. The goal of this school is to equip men and women to effectively perform the work that God has called them to do.

We live in a changing world. Nothing is the same as it was 50 years ago. Education has changed. Churches have changed. The world has changed. However, the gospel of Jesus Christ has not changed! Many years ago no one really thought about earning a credible degree at home. Therefore many never had the opportunity to fulfill their potential. Many felt called and dreamed of ministry but never had the chance to train for ministry. Today our school makes an education at home a reality. It all depends on you - if you want it? Do you want it? Do you want your Bachelor's degree in Ministry? Would you like to earn a Master's degree or even a doctorate? You can…if you want to. This simply requires some desire and work. If you will supply the effort we can supply the courses and the guidance to move you along to the degree that might otherwise be impossible to obtain.

Our courses and degrees are on the cutting edge of what is fresh and new. You are not going to listen to tapes made by people that you've never heard of before. In our degree program you will study the most current books written by the world's leading authors. These books will enhance your life and current ministry. A degree from NTS prepares you for a more fulfilling life and broader ministry.

Are you ready? God is ready. If He has called you then He wants to use you in a great and mighty way. We are here to help you to be all that God wants you to be in ministry. The next step is yours. Join with others by enrolling in a Newburgh Theological Seminary program and begin your journey today as one who is willing to be "a workman that needeth not to be ashamed, rightly dividing the word of truth." (II Timothy 2: 15).

In Christ's Service
Dr. Glenn Mollette, President

Earning Your Degree From Home Is A Reality

The following is how it works:

Fill out the application. One may be enclosed with this catalog. If not please call and we'll send you one. Or, you may fill out the application found on our website. Or, you may call us and we will fill out the application over the telephone.

Send the application to us with you're application fee of $50.

Await a letter or call from our school. If you do not hear from us within seven days please email or call us about your application.

If you are accepted then you will be given instructions on how to proceed.

Order the textbooks.

Read the textbooks.

Do the papers/assignments found in this catalog or our website.

Send the papers to us via mail or email attachment.

Pay your tuition month by month.

We will grade your papers and return them to you.

After all the courses are taken and graded, and your tuition is paid, you will receive your degree.

It's that simple.

We look forward to hearing from you today. Don't put off fulfilling your dreams. Make the decision to move forward with your life. We are help to help you.

A Wonderful Opportunity!

Newburgh Theological Seminary makes it possible for you to pursue your degree at home. It is not always practical to pack up a family and move to another state or city. With our school you can earn the degree you need and continue caring for your ministry and loved ones right where you are. Our school has students from all different denominational backgrounds. We are a Bible teaching, Christ – centered school. We are America's premier long distance education Bible College and Seminary. Students from over the United States are fulfilling their educational goals and fulfilling their degrees from Newburgh.

Mission statement: "The purpose of Newburgh Theological Seminary is to provide effective Biblical, Christ-centered training for men and women who want to prepare for greater ministry". Our program of education is preparing people to do 21st century work based on the life and message of our 1st century Jesus and New Testament church.

Doctrinal statement: Newburgh Theological Seminary believes the Bible is the word of God. We believe without any reservation the inspiration of the Old and New Testaments. We believe God's word is without error and is God's revelation to mankind.

The programs at Newburgh Theological Seminary are designed according to the fundamental educational principles of reading, thinking and doing.

One of the most important benefits of our program is that you will be able to gain a ministry education comparable to that offered at more traditional schools with similar courses and programs, but at a fraction of the total cost. And since Newburgh Theological Seminary is a distance education institution, you will be able to study at your own pace, making it possible to earn the degree that might otherwise be out of your reach.

You will appreciate the freedom to study when and where you want to without semester or classroom deadlines. You study at your own pace. One of the many benefits of such a system is that you may discover that you are able to learn more than might otherwise be possible when pressured by unrealistic semester schedules.

When you are finished, you will proudly display your degree with the confidence that can only come through having comprehended new truth, and the gaining of greater knowledge. That's because our graduates are able to minister to others with the confidence that their ministry education really did prepare them to touch the lives of others in a positive way.

Who Should Consider Our Program?

- Individuals already in ministry who are seeking continuing and additional education through a very practical or professional program specifically designed to meet their needs.

- Those who do not want to spend thousands upon thousands of dollars on a traditional degree or do not need to attend a traditional Bible College or Seminary program, but are seeking an honorable and credible alternative such as Newburgh Theological Seminary and Newburgh College of the Bible.

- Individuals who have earned credits, certificates or degrees from a less recognized institution and wish to upgrade their educational credentials to a higher school like Newburgh Theological Seminary/Newburgh College of the Bible.

- College graduates who want to move forward seeking a credible, practical and straightforward approach to earning their graduate or doctoral degree in an appropriate area of ministry.

College and Graduate Schools

We Have a Program for Every Need!

Our school has different levels that serves a targeted area, and provides a ministry training and education program to meet every need. Please review the degree descriptions and then refer to the pages immediately following for specific details.

Continuing Studies!

We offer an excellent program for every student who wants to occasionally take a course to stay refreshed in God's word and ministry. These courses are modestly priced. Refer to the tuition information page. We offer certification when these courses are completed and the student fulfills the assignment to demonstrate they have read the textbook. This is an excellent way to demonstrate credibility in an area of study for your church or denomination.

School of Undergraduate Studies

We offer Associate and Bachelor degrees in Ministry, Biblical Studies and Christian Counseling, Christian Communications, Preaching and many other areas of concentration. Refer to the tuition page in regards to the cost of our bachelor's degrees

School of Graduate Studies

We offer the Doctor of Ministry, Doctor of Theology and Doctor of Philosophy (Ph.D.). Please refer to prospectuses listed in this book on these programs. Tuition fees are on the tuition information page.

God has a great plan for your life!
Begin the plan today!

Administration and Staff

Dr. Glenn Mollette, President
Dr. Mollette is a graduate of Georgetown College, Southern Seminary, Lexington Theological Seminary, Campbellsville University and Newburgh Theological Seminary. He has the B.A. M.Div. D.Min. D.D and Ph.D. Degrees
Dr. Mollette is the former President of the Kentucky Baptist Convention.
He has preached all over the United States and abroad. He is the author of eight books.

Dr. Steve Fitts, Ph.D. Southern Baptist Theological Seminary, Louisville, Kentucky. M.Div. Southern Baptist Theological Seminary.

Dr. Nevalon Mitchell Jr. D.Min. Presbyterian Seminary, Louisville, Kentucky.
Seven Units of Clinical Pastoral Education

Dr Ramesh Deosarran, D. Min. Adjunct
Nazarene Bible College, Kansas City, Missouri

Dr. Jim Highland, Vice President of Development
Georgetown College and Southern Seminary. B.A M.Div and
D.Min. degrees

Rev. Kerry Newburn, Adjunct
Rockford Illinois,
President, Illinois Missionary Baptist Conference

Tommy Milan, M.Div. Newburgh Theological Seminary
Ph.D. Candidate
Student Advisor

Carole Bartley Johnson, Vice President of Administration
     President of Women's Ministries and Curriculum
     Transylvania University, Georgetown College and Midway College
     B.A.

John Beanblossom – Communications

Dr. Art Christmas, Georgetown College and Southern Seminary
  B.A. M.Div and D.Min
 Author of Grief Counseling

Dr. Billy Davis, Evangelism and Pastoral Ministries
Best Selling Author, "How to Overcome the "I Can't Help It Syndrome.""

Dr. Samuel A. Arowralaju, Ph.D. Candidate
Trinity and Newburgh Theological Seminary

Dr. Andrew Teo, Ph.D. Candidate
Newburgh Theological Seminary

Dr. Bruce Hayes, Ph.D.
Newburgh Theological Seminary

Dr. Jim Gibson, D.Min.
  Adjunct
Professor of Ministry at Oakland City University,
Oakland City, Indiana

Carolyn Craig, B.A. English and Creative Writing

We have adjunct professors who work with our school from all over the United States.

Accreditation

Newburgh Theological Seminary presents to you the very finest in long distance education. The leaders in Biblical/Christian and educational publishing supply the textbooks that we use in our curriculum. Only the most excellent in Biblical and ministry training materials are utilized toward our degrees. These books and materials are books that you can find in use worldwide and are almost always listed on Amazon.com or can be bought even at your local bookstore. You will not be supplied with materials presented by instructors you have never heard of and may not have any credentials themselves! You will study the best books and the finest authors in their area of ministry expertise. Once you have completed your course of study you will truly have learned something from some of the greatest and most credible instructors of our era.

Our school meets all the standards required of not for profit 501 © 3 religious schools in the state of Indiana. The groups that accredit Harvard or Yale do not accredit us nor can we afford to be. Accreditation is expensive. Schools such as these charge tuition's of $30,000 to $40,000 a year. We are not in this work to financially devastate people but to prepare and train people for ministry.

Every school that is accredited at one time was unaccredited. There is a long process to accreditation and accreditation is not required to provide ministry and Biblical training. Even recognized accreditation does not assure a quality education. There are many schools that have accreditation but aren't very credible when it comes to providing Biblical and ministry training. While they may have a large campus and large tuitions they may not have much credibility in providing sound training for doing Christian work. Therefore many will attend these schools and still graduate with a poor education. Schools such as these are known widely by churches and peers and ministry groups and can often reflect on an individual. Our school offers the finest in theological and ministry training. A degree from our school is worth something because the textbooks and ministry tools that every student studies are from scholars and professionals who are very thoroughly trained in their fields.

Will my degree be accepted? This depends on you. A degree is never worth more than the person who has the degree. Many students have graduated from schools where thousands of dollars were spent to obtain the education. Yet after the student graduated they still had very little knowledge of God's word and had grown very little in their ministry skills. While they had an accredited degree to hang on the wall they went on to do very little in ministry because they did not have the skills that churches and schools look for when hiring someone and that is ability which can only come from credible teaching and training. Our school will continue to shy away from any kind of accreditation that might weaken our ability to train men and women to be effective servants of Christ in their church and place of ministry service. Few pastors are promoted to bigger churches simply because of the name of their institution. Churches want ministers who demonstrate that they truly have a real degree and education by what they are and how they perform their tasks. A degree from Newburgh Theological Seminary and Newburgh College of the Bible will give you the credible degree that you need but most importantly you will engage in the studies that will sharpen your God-given talents to do great things for God. Your church and peers will accept your degree if they accept you. The degree does not make the person. The person makes the degree.

Another question often asked is "Will a degree from NTS be accepted by another school?" This all depends on the school. No school has to accept credit from any other school. In many cases the credit from NTS should be acceptable to any other school. We utilize only the finest material available. However, we cannot say what another school will accept.

The main question to be asked when considering a school is this the school that will please God? If it pleases God then it doesn't matter who is displeased. We ask all of our students to pray about all that they do in life. Our school is about honoring Christ and being His servants. We feel the accreditation of God is on our school because all we do strives to please Him in academics and ministry training.

If the school is right for God then it's right for you. We encourage you to prayerfully fill out the application form and send it back to us as soon as possible so that you may begin today to prepare for the greater ministry that God has for you!

Accelerated Seminary Degree

Please inquire about the courses that are offered around the country throughout the year. Some of these will be in the Newburgh/Evansville, Indiana area. Others will be offered in other states. Please call us at (812) 858 – 3920 to inquire about our next accelerated schedule. Also, check out our website at www.newburghseminary.com

Most schedules offer classes on Thursday/Friday or Friday night/ Saturday morning. Sometimes you may be able to earn credit for two to four classes depending on the schedule. These courses are not necessary for graduation. A student never has to leave home to earn a degree from our school. However, classes are offered so that a student may accelerate the process.

Bachelor Degrees

The Bachelor degree programs of NTS are 120 hours. However, life credit is given for years of ministry, military or work related experience. Please talk with an advisor from the school to determine exactly what your needs are for your degree completion.

We have several degrees:

Bachelor of Biblical Studies

Bachelor of Ministry

Bachelor of Christian Counseling

Bachelor of Theology

Bachelor of Christian Creative Writing

Bachelor of Christian Education

We also have other Bachelor degrees that may be what you are looking for.
Please call and we will do everything we can to help you to earn the degree that is right for you.
(812) 858 – 3920   Email is newburghseminary@aol.com

Bachelor of Theology
Newburgh Theological Seminary

Purpose

The purpose of this degree is to acquaint the student with a broad perspective of Christian theology.

Requirements

This degree requires 120 hours. Ninety hours of life experience credit may be granted. Thirty hours of courses are necessary to graduate. Six five-hour courses must be completed to obtain the degree. All course work may be emailed to NewburghSeminary@aol.com or mailed to the school address at Newburgh Seminary, P.O. Box 1238, Newburgh, Indiana 47629. Assignments mailed to the school should always be accompanied with a self addressed stamped envelope so that the work may be returned.

Curriculum

    The Case for Christ by Lee Strobel
    Christian Theology by Millard J. Erickson
    Bible Doctrine by Jeff Purswell
    A History of the Christian Church by Williston Walker
    The Heart of Christianity: Rediscovering a Life of Faith by Marcus J. Borg
    Mere Christianity by C.S. Lewis
    Basic Theology: A Popular Systematic Guide to Understanding Biblical Truth by Charles Caldwell Ryrie

    Each book is orderable via Amazon.com or your local bookstore.
    After the book is read complete the following:
      Summarize your favorite chapter in the book in three to five pages.
    Write at least a paragraph as to what each chapter in the book is about.

How may this book be of help to you in your Christian life and ministry? What is one thing that you learned from this book that stands out as something totally different than what you had ever thought of before? What is something this book affirmed in your life?

Bachelor of Biblical Studies
Newburgh Theological Seminary

Purpose: The purpose of the Bachelor of Biblical studies is to give the student an overall basic understanding of the Old and New Testaments.

Degree Requirements - 120 hours fulfilled through course work and life credit. There must be at least 30 hours of course work.

Six of the following textbooks may be chosen for academic fulfillment.
Each book constitutes five hours of credit or one course. The book should be read and studied for understanding. A five to twenty page paper should be written on each book.
The following should be addressed in each paper:

1. The title of the book
2. The author of the book
3. Chapter titles in the book
4. Summarize briefly what each chapter is about.
5. Write out five to ten truths or concepts you learned in the book.
6. How might this book benefit you in your life or ministry?
7. Is there anything in this book that you had already studied or had learned in your life work? Explain?

Select six of the following books. Each book will serve as one course for this degree.
Books are orderable through your local bookstore or Amazon.com

Encountering The Old Testament: A Christian Survey by Bill T. Arnold
A Survey of Old Testament Introduction by Archer Gleason, Jr.
30 Days to Understanding the Bible in 15 Minutes a Day by Max Anders
The Bible From Scratch: The New Testament for Beginners by Donald L. Griggs
Encountering The New Testament: A Historical and Theological Survey by Walter L. Elwell
The Bible Jesus Read by Phillip Yancey
Who Wrote The Bible by Richard E. Friedman
The Secret Teachings of Jesus by Marvin Meyer
Introducing The New Testament by John William Drane
The Epistle to the Romans by Leon Morris

Papers may be submitted via mail to Newburgh Theological Seminary, P.O. Box 1238, Newburgh, Indiana 47629. Please include a SASE if you wish to have your paper returned.
Or, preferably submit by email.

Bachelor of Christian Counseling

Newburgh Theological Seminary

Introduction:

The Bachelor program consists of courses that will enable the student to become better equipped in Christian counseling.

Required: The Bachelor program consists of 120 hours but up to 90 hours of life learning credit may be given toward this degree.

Six five-hour courses on top of life-learning credit are necessary to receive the Bachelor of Christian Counseling.

The courses consist of at least one textbook per course. After reading the textbook the student should respond as follows:
1. Ten to fifteen pages to summarize the book.
2. Point out practical principles that you can utilize in your Christian service
3. What are major themes of the book

Papers should be typed and submitted to NewburghSeminary@aol.com via email attachment or mailed to the school address.

Any six of the following textbooks may be chosen.
The student may suggest two alternate textbooks to be approved by a faculty advisor.

> Textbooks are available via most major bookstores or Amazon.com
> Competent Christian Counseling by Timothy Clinton/ George W. Ohlschlager

> The Practice of Spiritual Direction by William A. Barry

> Modern Psychotherapies A Comprehensive Christian Appraisal by Stanton L. Jones

> Silent Struggler by Glenn Mollette

> Biblical Directionism by Dr. Dennis Frey

> Basic Christian Leadership by John W. Stott

> Released From Shame: Moving beyond the pain of the past by Sandra D. Wilson

> Theology of Christian Counseling by Jay Edward Adams

> Nursing Home Nightmares by Glenn Mollette

Bachelor of Ministry
Newburgh Theological Seminary

The purpose of this degree is to broaden the student's perspectives and understanding of Christian ministry.

Requirements

The Bachelor's degree program requires 120 hours. Ninety hours of study are granted for either previous education or life experience credit. Thirty hours of course work must be taken before the degree is granted. Currently six five-hour courses constitute the thirty hours needed.

Curriculum

Students are encouraged to take one course at a time. Although all books may be ordered at once. All books are orderable via most bookstores or Amazon.com

The following textbooks are appropriate for this degree. For this particular degree one textbook serves as a course. The name of the course is the name of the textbook.

The Purpose Driven Church by Rick Warren
Courageous Leadership by Bill Hybels
Spiritual Leadership: Principles of Leadership for Every Believer by J. Oswald Sanders
Servant Leader by Ken Blanchard
Revolution in Leadership: Training Apostles for Tomorrow's Church by
Reggie McNiel
The Emotionally Healthy Church by Peter Scazzero
Connecting Your Heart to Others: 6 Small Group Lessons on Fellowship by Doug Fields
Letters to Timothy: A Handbook for Pastors by John R. Bisagno
Six of the previous books may be chosen.
Once the book is read the student should summarize the book. This may take five to ten pages.

The student should state in one to two pages how this book could be beneficial in ministry.

One half page should be written about how this book may have changed the student's perspective or affirmed something the student already knew about ministry.

The paper for each book may be submitted to Newburghseminary@aol.com or mailed to Newburgh Theological Seminary, P.O. Box 1238, Newburgh, Indiana 47629 Please always include a SASE for return of assignments.

Bachelor of Creative Writing
Newburgh Theological Seminary

Purpose: The Purpose of this degree is to acquaint the degree candidate with a broader understanding and experience of the art of creative writing.

This degree is 120 hours. Life learning and writing projects may allow the candidate up to 90 hours of exemption. At least 30 hours of study must be completed with NTS.

Up to six of the following textbooks may be chosen for this degree.
Each textbook should be ordered via your local bookstore or Amazon.com. When the textbook is read the student should write a paper addressing the following:
1. What are ten major themes of the book?
2. Name five new principles that you learned in this study?
3. Summarize the chapter that made the greatest impression on you and tell why it did.
4. What down each chapter title and summarize the chapter in two to three paragraphs.
5. When all six textbooks are read and the above papers are submitted the student must submit a creative writing paper of ten to twenty pages. This paper should follow the rules learned in the study. The story may be fictional, nonfiction…. or anything that the student wishes to write about.

Suggested curriculum:
On Writing Well, 25th Anniversary: The Classic Guide to   Writing Nonfiction by William K. Zinsser
Writing Alone and With Others by Pat Schneider and Peter Elbow
A Manual For Writing Term Papers, Theses and   Dissertations by Kate L. Turabian
Writing Down The Bones: Freeing The Writer Within by Natalie Goldberg
Writing Fiction: The Practical Guide From New York's Acclaimed Creative Writing School by Gotham Writer's Workshop
Writing Alone and With Others by Pat Schneider, Peter Elbow
Writing Creative Nonfiction: Instruction and Insights from Teachers of the Associated Writing Programs
The Right to Write: An Invitation and Initiation into the Writing Life by Julia Cameron

All papers should be submitted to NewburghSeminary@aol.com as an attachment. Most papers are graded and returned within a week. Or snail address is NTS, P.O. Box 1238, Newburgh, Indiana 47629.
Telephone number is 812 858-3920.

If you mail your paper please send a SASE for your paper's return.

Graduation is held in May of each year. You may participate or have your degree mailed to you.

Bachelor of Christian Education
Newburgh Theological Seminary

The Bachelor of Christian Education degree provides the student with a foundational level of courses for basic understanding of the nature of Christian Education.

This degree requires 120 hours of credit. Up to 90 hours of credit may be given for living learning experience, ministry experience, military experience or transfer of credit from another school. Thirty hours of study or six courses must be taken to earn this degree.

Books for each course must be read with the following assignment for each textbook:
- What are the five most impressive truths or concepts you learned from the book?
- Summarize each chapter of the book in one to two pages.
- Explain in one page how this book may help you in your future Christian education endeavors

Please select six of the following textbooks to utilize toward your degree fulfillment:

- Introducing Christian Education: Foundations for the 21st Century by Michael J. Anthony
- The Case for Classical Christian Education by Douglas Wilson
- Administration of the Christian School by Roy W. Lowrie
- Personnel Administration in the Christian School by Lester Brubaker
- Christian Counseling A Comprehensive Guide By Gary Collins
- Christian Coaching: Helping Others Turn Potential Into Reality by Gary Collins
- Mapping Christian Education: Approaches to Congregational Learning by Jack L. Seymour
- Teaching the Bible to Adults and Youth by Dick Murray and Lyle Schaller
-

Master Degrees

The Master degree may be pursued after completion of the bachelor's degree.

The following degrees are offered by NTS.

Master of Divinity – 90 credit hours

Master of Biblical Studies – 30 credit hours

Master of Ministry – 30 credit hours

Master of Theology – 30 credit hours
(In development – should be ready by the time you
receive this catalog)

Master of Christian Counseling – 30 credit hours

Master of Christian Education

Please consult with your NTS advisor about these and other Master degrees offered by our school

You may call us (812) 858 – 3920 or email us at newburghseminary@aol.com

Master of Divinity
Newburgh Theological Seminary

Introduction:

This degree gives the student an overall education that is suitable for Ministry preparation. This degree will acquaint the student with New and Old Testament studies as well as familiarize the student with Philosophy, Ethics, Evangelism, Pastoral studies and Biblical Preaching along with opportunities for the student to select electives.

This degree is 90 hours or approximately 18 courses.
All textbooks are orderable from most major bookstores or
Amazon.com.

Each course consists of at least one outstanding book that the student shall read to complete the course.

Upon ordering and reading the assigned book the student should summit the following information in writing (preferably typed) to Newburgh Seminary. We prefer that papers be sent as email attachments. However, if necessary they may be mailed to our address.

The information per assigned book is as follows:
A five to ten page summary of the textbook.
This paper should include: Up to ten truths learned from the book…how this book is beneficial to further ministry…what is the overall most important element of the book in your opinion and how will your reading better equip you to do God's work.

Some of the textbooks to fulfill this degree are as follows:
New Testament studies: Please note only 18 of the following classes/books are needed. The following list are books/classes that the student may choose from to fulfill the Master of Divinity degree.
Also the student may offer up to four electives to fulfill this degree of books that are not on any of our lists with advisor approval.

New Testament: Encountering the New Testament: A Historical and Theological Survey By Walter A. Elwell

Survey of the New Testament By Robert Horton

The Gospel in Brief by Leo Tolstoy

Nelson's New Testament Survey: Discover the Background, Theology and Meaning of Every Book in the NT By Mark Bailey

Essentials of New Testament Greek: A Student's Guide by Steven L. Cox

Encountering the Book of Romans: A Theological Survey by Douglas J. Moo Walter A. Elwell

Jesus The Messiah: A Survey of the Life Of Christ By Robert H. Stein

Paul: Missionary Theologian: A Survey of His Missionary Labours and Theology Robert L. Raymond

Linguistics for Students of New Testament Greek: A survey of basic concepts and applications by David Alan

John: Beloved Disciple a Survey of His Theology by Robert L. Reymond

The Lukan Passion Narrative: The Markan Material in Luke 22, 54-23,25, A Historical Survey; by Jay M. Harrington

Old Testament courses:
Survey of the Old Testament By Andrew E. Hill

Old Testament Hebrew Vocabulary: Learn on the Go by Jonathan T. Pennington (Audio CD)

Reading the Old Testament: An Introduction to the Hebrew Bible (with CD ROM) by Barry L. Bandstra

Encountering the Old Testament:
A Christian Survey by Bill T. Arnold

The Faith of Israel: A Theological Survey Of the Old Testament by William J. Dumbrell

The Minor Prophets By James E. Smith

Other NT courses:
1 & 2 Timothy and Titus: To Guard the Deposit by R.Kent, Hughes, Bryan Chapell

The Epistle to the Romans New International Commentary on the New Testament) By Douglas J. Moo

Epistle to the Hebrews by F.F. Bruce
The First Epistle to the Corinthians by Gordon D. Fee
The First and Second Epistles to the Thessalonians by Leon Morris
The Letter to the Ephesians by Peter T. O'Brien

Preaching Courses:
        Power in the Pulpit: How to Prepare and Deliver Expository Sermons by Jerry Vines

Annointed Expository Preaching By Stephen F. Olford

Preaching Through the Christian Year Fred B. Craddock

Preaching with Freshness by Bruce Mawhinney, Jay Adams

Inspired Preaching: A Survey of Preaching found in the New Testament by Richard C. Wells

Christian Philosophy
   Philosophical Foundations for a Christian Worldview By J.P. Moreland, William L. Craig

Works of Love: Kierkegaard's Writings By Soren Kierkegaard

The Christian Philosophy of Thomas Aquinas By Etienne Gilson

The Purpose Driven Life, Rick Warren

Will and Spirit: A contemplative Psychology by Gerald G. May

   Ethics
There's No Such Thing as "Business" Ethics:
There's only one rule for making decisions by John C. Maxwell

Readings in Christian Ethics: Issues and Applications by David K. Clark

The Common Good and Christian Ethics By David Hollenbach

The Complete C.S. Lewis Signature Classics by C.S. Lewis

Saintly Solutions to Life's Common Problems:
From Anger, Boredom, and Temptation to Gluttony, Gossip, and Greed by Joseph M. Esper

   Evangelism

Share Jesus Without Fear by William Frey
Talking about Jesus without Sounding Religious by Rebecca Manley

The Art of Personal Evangelism: Sharing Jesus in a Changing Culture by Will McRaney, Jr.

How to Share Your Faith by Greg Laurie
The Soul Winner by Charles H. Spurgeon
Five Steps to Sharing Your Faith by Bill Bright

Drawing the Net: 30 Practical Principles for Leading Others to Christ Publicly and Personally by O.S. Hawkins

Master of Biblical Studies

Newburgh Theological Seminary

This degree provides an opportunity for the student to pursue courses that will broaden Biblical understanding and perspective at the Master's level.

Requirements for admission: A Bachelor's degree from an approved institution.
    Prior Biblical training/education
    A goal for future ministry service
    Approval by the seminary board of advisors

Required for graduation:
    30 hours of credit or six five- hour classes

Available courses:
These books are available via most national bookstores or Amazon.com
Each book is a current course title for this degree program. Fulfillment of the
Course involves reading the book and responding as follows:
    Summarizing the book. Summarizing each chapter best does this.
    Close to at least one page per chapter summary showing that the book has been read and understood will be acceptable when submitting the paper for grading back to NewburghSeminary@aol.com. After the completion of each book the paper should be submitted for grading.

Suggested textbooks: Pick at least six to fulfill the 30 required hours.
Making Sense of Your World: A Biblical Worldview by Gary W. Phillips
30 Days to Understanding the Bible in 15 minutes a day by Max Anders
Encountering the New Testament: A Historical and Theological Survey by Walter A. Elwell
Grasping God's Word by J. Scott Duvall
Abraham: A Journey to the Heart of Three Faiths by Bruce Feiler
Introduction to Biblical Interpretation by William W. Klein
The Jesus I Never Knew by Phillip Yancey
The Tabernacle by David Levy
Who Wrote The Bible? By Richard E. Friedman
Six courses may be selected from these suggestions and up to three alternate studies may be offered by the student in writing to the seminary.

Master of Ministry
Newburgh Theological Seminary

This program enables the student to expand his academic and practical knowledge in ministry.

Requirements
    A Bachelor's degree from an approved school is required, plus
    Seminary approval.

Course requirements: 30 hours of study
    Six five-hour courses

Student may choose from the following classes:
    Servant Leader by Ken Blachard
    Courageous Leadership by Bill Hybels
    The Wounded Healer by Henri J. M. Nouwen
    Purpose Driven Church by Rick Warren
    Spiritual Leadership: Principles of Leadership for Every Believer by Oswald Sanders
    Can We Do That? By Andy Stanley
    Dictionary of Pastoral Care and Counseling by Rodney J. Hunter
    In The Name of Jesus: Reflections on Christian Leadership by Henri J.M. Nouwen

Each book is to be read and summarized. Each book constitutes a course. When the book is completed the student should try to summarize each chapter in about one page. These are to be submitted to the seminary via email attachment or mail for grading.

Master of Christian Counseling

Newburgh Theological Seminary

This degree will enable the student to develop to another level in the field of Christian counseling.

Bachelor's degree from an approved school is required for admission.
Approval by the seminary committee is also required.

Requirements:
A minimum of six five-hour courses.
Ten three page papers describing actual counseling or dialogues sessions.
These sessions do not have to be formal counseling hours but time spent with someone in a helpful situation.
All work should be typed and submitted to Newburgh Seminary via email attachment or mail.
A paper on each book should be submitted to the school. These papers should be a minimum of five pages and should include the following:
An overview all summary of the book.

A summary of your favorite chapter in the book.
The valuable truths that you have learned from each book. This could be one or two or several.
How you feel this book might be helpful to you in future Christian counseling.

Possible textbooks
The student may suggest up to three not found on our list.

All books are orderable via most bookstores or Amazon.com

The Biblical Basis of Christian Counseling for People Helpers: Relating the Basic Teachings of Scripture to People's Problems by Gary R. Collins
Competent Christian Counseling by Timothy Clinton

Psychology, Theology and Spirituality in Christian Counseling by Mark R. McMinn

The Healing Path: How the Hurts in Your Past Can Lead You to a More Abundant Life By Dan B. Allender

Silent Stuggler: A Caregiver's Personal Story By Glenn Mollette

Nursing Home Nightmares by Glenn Mollette

Biblical Directionism by Dr. Dennis Frey

Door of Hope, Recognizing and Resolving The Pains of Your Past, by Jan Frank

Master of Christian Education
Newburgh Theological Seminary

The Master of Christian Education degree guides the student through an advanced level of courses for continued development of the understanding of the nature of Christian Education.

This degree requires thirty hours of study or six graduate courses.

Books for each course must be read with the following assignment for each textbook:
- What are the five most impressive truths or concepts you learned from the book?
- Summarize each chapter of the book in one to two pages.
- Explain in one page how this book may help you in your future Christian education endeavors

Please select six of the following textbooks to utilize toward your degree fulfillment:

- Mind Siege: The Battle for the Truth by Tim Lahaye
- Building An Effective Church School: Guide for the Superintendent and Board of Christian Education by Kenneth D. Blazer
- The Effective Teacher: A Christian's Guide To Teaching by Bennie E. Goodwin
- Effective Christian School Management by James W. Deuink
- Five Dynamic Dimensions for Effective Teaching by Kevin Treston
- Effective Bible Teaching by Betty A. Carroll
- The God-Bearing Life: The Art of Soul Tending for Youth Ministry by Kenda Creasy Dean
- Christian Education Handbook by Bruce P. Powers

Doctoral Degrees

The following doctoral degrees are available from Newburgh Theological Seminary.

Doctor of Ministry - 45 credit hours and ministry project

Doctor of Theology – 45 credit hours and doctoral paper

Doctor of Philosophy (Ph.D.) – 45 credit hours and dissertation

We have Ph.D. degrees available in Biblical Studies, Theology, Ministry, Christian Counseling, Preaching, Evangelism and other ministry related fields.

Doctor of Ministry
Newburgh Theological Seminary

Introduction:

This degree is granted to the student who demonstrates a concentrated emphasis in ministry. The degree program is intended for students who have completed Bachelor's and Master's degrees and wish to increase their ministry skills academically and in practical application.

The Doctor of Ministry Project

The candidate must submit in writing his or her intended focus for the program. For example this may be most anything that applies to Christian life or ministry.

Examples are:

Doing Pastoral Care Through Preaching
Developing an Evangelistic Church
How to better organize the church administratively
Christian Counseling.

There are many, many possibilities and the doctoral candidates idea should be simply submitted to the seminary for consideration and approval.

There are six courses required before writing the Doctor of Ministry paper that should be fifteen to twenty pages in length. Three courses may be chosen by the candidate if they are supportive of the ministry paper he or she is writing.

The paper should address the following:

The purpose of the paper/project.
What was learned via the reading in preparation for the project?
What practical application did the student make during the actual doctoral project.
How was the course of study applied in life and ministry?
How will this study benefit the doctoral student in future ministry?
Any life examples and situations should be written up in the paper to illustrate truths learned or applied during the study.

This paper may be started at the beginning of the program. However, it should not be turned in until the six courses have been taken and papers submitted on each course. Each book read should have a five page paper type written and submitted explaining what was read and learned during the reading of each book.

Suggested books to order

All books are orderable via most bookstores or Amazon.com

Leading Congregational Change: A Practical Guide for the Transformational Journey by Jim Herrington

The Shape of Practical Theology: Empowering Ministry with Theological Praxis by Ray Sherman Anderson

Practicing Gospel: Unconventional Thoughts on the Church's Ministry by Edward Farley

The Effective Pastor: A Practical Guide to the Ministry by Robert C. Anderson

Multiply The Ministry: A Practical Guide for Grassroots Ministry Empowerment by Sean P. Reynolds

Effective Church Leadership: A Practical Sourcebook by Harris W. Lee

The Soul of Ministry: Forming Leaders for God's People by Ray S. Anderson

Doctor of Theology/Doctor of Philosophy

Requirements: Student must have a Bachelor and Master's degrees before applying for admission to either of these programs.

Application may be made via the official application form or by going to our website at www.newburghseminary.com and downloading the application form. Or, a student may apply over the phone at (812) 858 – 3920.

The Doctor of Theology/Ph.D. candidate will have the opportunity to grow in theological perspectives and understanding. Six of the following courses may be selected for the Th.D. program. The Ph.D. program requires eight of the following courses.

A student may suggest up to three alternate textbooks for the Th.D. and up to four alternate textbooks for the Ph.D.
These textbooks should be submitted in writing via mail or email to Newburgh Theological Seminary.

Textbooks should be read.
A paper on each textbook requires the following:
- A seven to ten page survey of what the book in your opinion says
- Include in your paper the top five themes that caught your attention and why they did.
- Include in your paper how this book will be useful to you in your future Christian work?
- Include how this book will help you, if any, toward preparation toward your dissertation?

Suggested textbooks:

Systematic Theology By Wayne A. Gruden

The Heart of Christianity: Rediscovering a Life of Faith By Marcus J. Borg

Christian Theology by Millard J. Erickson

The God Who Risks: A Theology Of Providence by John Sanders

A Search for the Spiritual: Exploring Real Christianity by James Emery

Experiencing the Passion of Jesus By Lee Strobel, Garry Poole

It's Not About Me: Rescue from the Life We Thought Would Make Us Happy by Max Lucado

The Story of Christian Theology: Twenty Centuries of Tradition & Reform By Roger E. Olson

The Spirit of Early Christian Thought: Seeking the Face of God By Robert Louis Wilken

Mere Christianity By C.S. Lewis

Dissertation:

Doctor of Philosophy (Ph.D.)

Newburgh Theological Seminary

Ph.D. in Christian Counseling

Introduction:

The purpose of the Ph.D. program in Christian counseling is to enable the student to concentrate his studies in this area of ministry with deeper understanding and concepts. The core courses, counseling hours and Dissertation will demonstrate academic and practical understanding.

Core Courses: Biblical Directionism by Dr. Dennis Frey
      Silent Struggler by Dr. Glenn Mollette
      Nursing Home Nightmares by Dr. Glenn Mollette
      The Marriage Vows by Dr. Glenn Mollette
      (Cassette tape series…orderable via seminary)
      Christian Counseling A Comprehensive Guide by Gary R. Collins
      Psychology, Theology and Spirituality in Christian Counseling by Mark R. McMinn
      Competent Christian Counseling by Timothy George
      The Art of Christian Listening by Thomas N. Hart
      Boundaries in Marriage by Dr. Henry Cloud
      The Healing Path: How Hurts in your past can lead you to a more abundant life by Dan B. Allender
      Sex, Men and God: A Godly Man's Roadmap to Sexual Success by Dr. Doug Weiss
      The Practice of Spiritual Direction by William A. Barry
      (All books are available by order from most bookstores or Amazon.com)

The Dissertation:

The Dissertation theme should be submitted to Newburgh Seminary at the outset of study. This theme should be one pertaining to the candidate's studies. The theme should be one that can be addressed in the 50-page dissertation covering the subject matter in such a way that demonstrates academic research and practical application. Since Newburgh Seminary considers all doctoral projects for publication…the dissertation should be written for market or public consumption utilizing common English grammar and sentence style. All references should be footnoted with the footnotes and sources appearing at the end of the paper. The dissertation may be started at the beginning of the doctoral program but may not be turned in until the six core courses are completed. The candidate may suggest and substitute up to four courses that do not appear on this prospectus. However, Newburgh Seminary must approve these. Once the dissertation is submitted and approved the candidate will be awarded the Doctor of Philosophy (Ph.D.).

Doctor of Philosophy (Ph.D.) in Biblical Studies

Newburgh Theological Seminary

Requirements

The Ph.D. candidate must have a Bachelor's and Master's degree approved by our seminary before admission into the program is granted. The student must prove that he or she possesses the academic background capable of pursuing the Ph.D. degree. After consultation and review the Administrative faculty will determine if the candidate qualifies for admission. Once admission is granted the following pertains to the doctoral candidate.

Six core courses of study related to the doctoral field and one research dissertation that is at least 50 typed pages in length typed and double spaced with the font being no less than eleven and no larger than twelve. We ask that the common rules of English be followed in the written presentation of this paper.

The candidate may choose from any of the following courses for this program.
  The candidate is also welcome to suggest up to four books that he or she would wish to interchange with these books.

Every book should be read. These books do not include the student's list of books that will be used in writing the dissertation project. After each book is read for the six core courses a paper of at least ten pages should be presented with the following information:
1. List up to ten principles presented by the book.
2. Summarize at least one chapter of the book and explain why this chapter was meaningful to you
3. What was the strength of the book?
4. What was the area of less interest to you that you read in the book?
5. Explain what the overall theme of the book is about if it has one.
6. How, if any, will this book be useful to you in your future work or ministry?
7. Write up to three typed pages giving an overview of the book.

Suggested textbooks:
  Encountering The Book of Psalms: A Literary and Theological Introduction by C. Hassell Bullock
  Encountering The Old Testament: A Christian Survey by Bill T. Arnold
  The Bible in English by David Daniell
  30 Days to Understanding the Bible in Fifteen Days by Max E.
  The Second Most Important Book You Will Ever Read by Dan Patrick
  Encountering The New Testament by Walter Elwell
  The Complete Dead Sea Scrolls in English by Geze Vermes
  Ancient Christian Gospels: Their History and Their Development by Helmut Koester
  Jesus The Messiah by Donald Gutherie
  The Religion of Paul the Apostle by John Ashton
  The Jesus I Never Knew by Philip Yancey
  Old Testament Survey by William Sanford
  The Hermeneutical Spiral by Grant R. Osborne
  Basics of Biblical Greek Workbook by William D. Mounce

Dissertation guidelines:

The candidate's dissertation idea should be submitted in writing as soon as possible. The Biblical Studies student may wish to focus on a book or passage of scripture or theme in scripture. The dissertation should be written in such a way that it would be worthy or public consumption. Every dissertation submitted will be considered and read with the prospects of publication. While no student is required to publish the dissertation it is certainly a worthy way of preserving the student's work and in time possibly earning income from sales of the book.

The Dissertation should introduce the theme and then in detail research the theme and provide in lay language the exposition or details of the theme. Footnotes and research notes should be noted numerically after each quote with the source listed at the end of the paper. This paper may be started at the beginning of the doctoral program with approval of the advisor. It may not be turned in until the six cores courses are fulfilled.

Doctor of Philosophy (Ph.D.) in Pastoral Ministries

Newburgh Theological Seminary

Requirements:

The Ph.D. candidate must have a Bachelor's and Master's degree approved by our seminary before admission into the program is granted. The student must prove that he or she possesses the academic background capable of pursuing the Ph.D. degree. After consultation and review the Administrative faculty will determine if the candidate qualifies for admission. Once admission is granted the following pertains to the doctoral candidate.

Six core courses of study related to the doctoral field and one research dissertation that is at least 50 typed pages in length typed and double spaced with the font being no less than eleven and no larger than twelve. We ask that the common rules of English be followed in the written presentation of this paper. Please also see "books we recommend," in preparing research papers at the end of the doctoral section.

The candidate may choose from any of the following courses for this program.
The candidate is also welcome to suggest up to four books that he or she would wish to interchange with these books.

Every book should be read. These books do not include the student's list of books that will be used in writing the dissertation project. After each book is read for the six core courses a paper of at least ten pages should be presented with the following information:
1. List up to ten principles presented by the book.
2. Summarize at least one chapter of the book and explain why this chapter was meaningful to you
3. What was the strength of the book?
4. What was the area of less interest to you that you read in the book?
5. Explain what the overall theme of the book is about if it has one.
6. How, if any, will this book be useful to you in your future work or ministry?
7. Write up to three typed pages giving an overview of the book.

Dissertation Theme:
Developing a Healing Church for Hurting People
(This is one student's dissertation theme. We ask every student to develop their own dissertation theme).

Suggested textbooks:
Encountering The Book of Psalms: A Literary and   Theological Introduction by C. Hassell Bullock
Healing Hope for Bruised Souls by Mary Theresa Webb
Healing Church Abuse: How to Break Free from Bad Church Experiences by Ken Blue
Ministry and Community: Recognizing Community and Preventing Ministry Impairment by Len Sperry
Healing Relationships: Christians Manual of Lay Counseling by Stephan Grunlan
Beyond Forgiveness: The Healing Touch of Church Discipline by Don Baker
Healing of Memories: Prayer and Confession, Steps to Inner Healing by Matthew Linn
The Healing Church: Practical Programs for Health Ministries by Abigail Evans
Healing the Dysfunctional Church Family by David Mains
Churches That Heal: Becoming a Church that Mends Broken Hearts and Restores Shattered Lives by Doug Murren
The Miracle of Healing in Your Church Today by Jim Lynn

Dissertation guidelines:

The candidate's dissertation idea should be submitted in writing as soon as possible. The Biblical Studies student may wish to focus on a book or passage of scripture or theme in scripture. The dissertation should be written in such a way that it would be worthy or public consumption. Every dissertation submitted will be considered and read with the prospects of publication. While no student is required to publish the dissertation it is certainly a worthy way of preserving the student's work and in time possibly earning income from sales of the book.

The Dissertation should introduce the theme and then in detail research the theme and provide in lay language the exposition or details of the theme. Footnotes and research notes should be noted numerically after each quote with the source listed at the end of the paper. This paper may be started at the beginning of the doctoral program with approval of the advisor. It may not be turned in until the six cores courses are fulfilled.

Doctor of Philosophy
Newburgh Theological Seminary

Proclamation/Biblical Preaching

Introduction:

The Ph.D. program will enable the doctoral candidate to do an overall study of research and practice in the realm of Proclamation/preaching. The Ph.D. candidate will show in the writing dissertation the results of the research and what has been learned during the candidacy program. Average dissertation is between 50 to 100 pages. A bibliography should be a minimum of 15 books that the candidate has referred to in the preparation for writing the dissertation.

Expectation:

At the outset of the Ph.D. program the student will submit in writing via mail or email the focus or theme of the dissertation paper. After approval of the theme the dissertation may be pursued. This paper should be a minimum of 50 pages and suitable for publication.

When the seminary advisor approves the theme of the dissertation the student may also submit book titles that may be pursued in the preliminary study that is required before the paper is begun.

Six courses of study are required before the writing of the paper. These books may be selected from our suggested textbooks. The student may select up to three textbooks and should be submitted and approved by the Advisor.

A ten to fifteen page summary of each course/textbook should be submitted via mail or email as the doctoral candidate finishes them.

Suggested courses for the preliminary studies:

Available via your local bookstore or Amazon.com

Biblical Preaching: The Development and Delivery of Expository Messages by Haddon W. Robinson
Witness of Preaching by Thomas G. Long
Christ Centered Preaching: Redeeming the Expository Sermon by Bryan Chapell
The Four Pages of the Sermon by Paul Scott Wilson
Power in the Pulpit by Jerry Vines
Preaching That Changes Lives by Michael Fabarez
The 12 Essential Skills for Biblical Preaching by Wayne McDill

The Ph.D. program has no time restraints. However, we do encourage the completion of this program in two years.

Doctor of Philosophy (Ph.D.) in Christian Public Relations

Newburgh Theological Seminary

The purpose of this Ph.D. program is to provide an opportunity for in-depth study and research for the Ph.D. candidate in the realm of public relations and community service.

Six core courses of textbook studies are required before the writing of the Ph.D. dissertation. These studies will increase the awareness of the candidate in the realm of community service and opportunities for fulfilling the mission of Christ.

Suggested courses:
(The candidate may make textbook suggestions before the writing of the dissertation).

1. Christians As Partners: Information, Consultation and Public Participation in Policy Making by Joanne Caddy
2. The Quiet Hand of God: Faith-Based Activism and the Public Role of Mainline Protestantism by Robert Wuthnow
3. The Global Face of Public Faith: Politics, Human Rights and Christian Ethics (Moral Traditions) by David Hollenbach
4. How To Win The Culture War: A Christian Battle Plan for a Society in Crisis by Peter Kreeft
5. Executive Values: A Christian Approach To Organizational Leadership by Kurt Senske
6. The Right Questions: Truth, Meaning and Public Debate by Phillip E. Johnson
7. Ethics: Approaching Moral Decisions (Contours of Christian Philosophy) by Arthur F. Holmes
8. The Work of Christ (Contours of Christian Theology) by Robert Letham

Select six of the eight textbooks. You may suggest up to three of your own and three from these eight of you deem best for your dissertation.

Write a five to ten page summary on each book.

What is the theme of the book? Or…what are the themes of the book?

What was your favorite chapter in the book and why?

How will this book affect your ministry?

Was there anything that you read in the book that you have already experienced or practiced in public service or Christian ministry? Explain.

How will the reading of this book help you in writing your dissertation? Explain.

Dissertation:

The dissertation is the heart of the Ph.D. program. The dissertation should be 50 to 100 pages in length. The document should be typed and double-spaced utilizing the rules and grammar of the English language. The theme for the dissertation should be submitted before beginning the process of research. Once the theme is approved the candidate is encouraged to develop a list of at least anther ten textbooks or more that the candidate will research in preparation for writing the dissertation. A bibliography should demonstrate thorough study of the theme of the dissertation. These additional books are for the student's research and do not necessarily need approval by the seminary.

All papers may be submitted for grading via email attachment. Or they may be submitted by the US mail. If mailing papers please include a SASE. The dissertation may also be emailed via attachment. All dissertations are considered for worldwide publication and distribution.

Once the dissertation is read and approved by the seminary trustees then the Doctor of Philosophy degree will be granted. This degree may be awarded during graduation exercises or may be mailed to the candidate.

Dissertations

Dissertations, Doctor of Ministry project papers, and textbook reports.

We recommend the following book:
    A Manual for Writing Term Papers, Theses and Dissertations by Kate L. Turabian

Endorsement Certification

Newburgh College of the Bible and Theological Seminary offer opportunities to receive ministry certification in many areas.

Consider some of the following areas of ministry certificates that may be helpful to you.

Ministry Certification

Christian Counseling Certification

Preaching Certification

Youth Ministry Certification

Children's Ministry Certification

Mission's Certification

Preaching Certification

Evangelism Certification

Small Group/Bible Teacher Certification

Continuing Education Certification

Please call today and an advisor will talk to you about our endorsement certification opportunities. (812) 858 – 3920 or email us at newburghseminary@aol.com

Application

You may remove this form from this book
and mail it to us at:
Newburgh Theological Seminary
P.O. Box 1238, Newburgh, Indiana 47629
Or call us at (812) 858 – 3920.

Name:

Address:

Telephone

Email

Social Security Number

Birth date:

Past Education:

High School

College

Other

Life experience credit:
   ( ) Ministry - list number of years _____
   ( ) Military
   ( ) Volunteer church service - list number of years_____

Tuition

Please check the tuition supplement to this book for current tuition prices.
If you have questions about costs please call today and someone will answer your questions in regards to tuition.

Financial aid and scholarship assistance are sometimes available. Call and find out what might be available for you.

Our telephone number is (812) 858 – 3920

Mail application or any correspondence to:
Newburgh Seminary
P.O. Box 1238
Newburgh, Indiana 47629

Our website is www.newburghseminary.com

Email is newburghseminary@aol.com

Life Is Like Graduation

(Delivered by Dr. Glenn Mollette to a graduating class)

Hebrews 11: 8 – 10:

"By faith, Abraham, when called to go to a place he would later receive as his inheritance, obeyed and went, even though he did not know where he was going. By faith he made his home in the promised land like a stranger in a foreign country; he lived in tents, as did Isaac and Jacob, who were heirs with him of the same promise. For he was looking forward to the city with foundations, whose architect and builder is God."

What graduation do you remember the most? Was it from junior high, high school, college or a graduate school? Today may be the graduation that you will remember most of all!

Abraham is a character in the Bible who experienced graduation but it was different than what we are observing.

Abraham graduated from one land to another. He graduated in location. He graduated to new experiences. He graduated to new challenges. He graduated on to different adversities. He graduated on to failures. He graduated on to blessings and victories.

Let's briefly consider his location. He leaves behind the land of Haran and sets out for Canaan. Haran was not the land God had for his people. He had a better land for them – the land of promise. It would be the land of Canaan.

We all go through location changes. Graduation may or may not bring about a change of location. Most of you are from different towns and will move on to different towns in the years ahead. God has been at work preparing you for something greater and bigger. It may be now a great move on to bigger things. Or, maybe now he will be able to use you right where you are for bigger things.

Life is filled with one location and one opportunity after another. New locations, opportunities and environments can be challenging but they can also be exciting with new and great opportunities.

Abraham would graduate on to new experiences. His experiences would be almost unreal. Becoming a father at an age when most people are dead with a woman too old to have a child. Inheriting a land that would become sacred to his descendants.

God has for every follower new blessings and new mercies and grace far greater than our sins. Have you graduated on to new experiences with God? Or, is your life and walk with God like high school graduation a happy, but distant memory? God wants us to love him and experience him but like Abraham we move on to new encounters and blessings.

Abraham moved on to new challenges. He moved on to new adversities.

In the land of Haran there was the challenge of culture and evil. Abraham would still face challenges in the future. He would have to deal with his nephew Lot who had a problem of living way too close to sin and immorality in Sodom and Gomorrah. There is the story where Abraham and Sarah went down into Egypt to

41

escape a famine in Canaan and Abraham lied about Sarah being his wife and said she his sister in order to save his own skin. And it brought such plague upon the King Abimelech who had not even slept yet with Sarah that he gave her back to Abraham with a firm scolding to Abraham for doing such a crazy thing. Abandoning his wife…lying about his relationship with her.

Graduation represents the end of one challenge. But new challenges are always ahead.

However, you have proven that you can arise to the challenge. You have studied, worked, prayed and carried out the Lord's will in regards to your education. You have led churches and worked jobs while you burned the midnight oil and earned your degree at home. God will bless you for you diligence.

Abraham went from a challenging land to other challenges. But God saw Abraham through. Abraham while challenged was trying to follow the call of God upon his life. He made mistakes but he had a relationship with God that saw him through his challenges and adversities. How are you going to face yours? Are you really smart? Well, it helps to be smart. But to every life there are challenges that you cannot handle without the help and the hand of God. God led Abraham out of Haran and took care of him all the way.

Abraham moved on to blessings. He and Sarah would inherit a beautiful land and the Bible says in Hebrews 11: 12 "And so from this one man, and he as good as dead, came descendants as numerous as the stars in the sky and as countless as the sand on the seashore."

My prayer for each graduate today is that you will move on to those blessings that God has for you as numerous as the stars in the sky.

God had a blessing for Abraham and Sarah and they got the blessing. But it didn't come without their obedience to God.

Yes God wants a heart that loves him. God wants a heart that is faithful to him and God wants a life that will obey him. There is no other way to be happy in Jesus but to trust and obey. And Abraham trusted and obeyed.

One big word stands out over the life of Abraham – unknown.
1. The unknown is scary
I think he trusted all the way. He was willing to make a decision. He was willing to go to a land that he did not have a clue as to where he was going. Your company says, you get into the car and head West and we will call you and tell you where to stop. That's about what it was like for Abraham and Sarah. And then when God gave Abraham a son he told him to take him out and kill him as a sacrifice. Abraham trusted God but that had to be such an unknown for Abraham.

Today you are here as living proof that you trusted God to lead you with your education and degree. He led you to our school. Through correspondence and email and long distance studying you did the assignments and now you are graduating today with your degree! To God be the glory!

What will this time next year bring? For thousands of people all over America and the world they will still be staring at one of our advertisements or reading our catalog. They will still only be dreaming and wishing they had their degree. But you made the decision and carried it forth with dedication. You have completed the goal that you had! Surely this is a wonderful feeling for you today!

2ndly the unknown is unpredictable. No one can predict the future for sure.
Abraham had no real clue as to what he was getting himself into for sure…except he knew that God was with him, and that's what really mattered.

42

3rd The unknown asks questions such as When, how, how long how much, why?

How long will this trip take and how much will it cost and why do I have to make this journey?

Why do I have to go to boot camp? Why do I have spend time taking courses in a long distance college or graduate school? Why nine months of pregnancy? Why is this illness so long, why did my love one have to die? And why when you think its bad enough it gets worse when you really didn't think it could? And then we wonder, what's next?

Graduation day came for Abraham. Time to graduate on to new challenges and new opportunities. And that's not bad because four years of high school can be fun but you don't want to stay there forever. You don't want to be 28 and still in high school. Good things come to an end and we move on to new chapters even if they are sometimes scary. A year or two years of seminary or Bible College are incredibly fulfilling. They are a gigantic blessing. But you don't want to spend all your life trying to earn your seminary or Bible degree. You want the study. You want the education. You want the degree and then it's time to move on! Today you are graduating and moving on! To God be the glory!

With Abraham Faithfulness and obedience paid. They paid for Joseph. Joseph was always being knocked down and bad things were happening to him but he still couldn't keep from being blessed and coming out of it.

He was thrown into a pit. Poor Joseph. Betrayed by his brothers, poor Joseph, sold into slavery poor Joseph. He is accused of rape, poor Joseph, thrown into prison, poor Joseph. But even in Jail Joseph was faithful and God blessed him and elevated him and eventually in life he was second only in prominence and wealth to the Pharoah of Egypt.

God sometimes blesses in mysterious ways. Someday when we are in heaven we will look back and say that was a mysterious way that God worked in my life. I can look back and see how God worked. I couldn't see it then. But look at all that I have in heaven today.

Abraham couldn't see where he was going but look how he was blessed because he was obedient to God.

I have three doctorates. Don't cringe. I'm not bragging. One of them is from The Lexington Theological Seminary and for almost three years I wrote papers and did research and prayed and fasted before I received the degree. On the paper that I have it says, this degree is conferred with all the rights, honors and privileges which pertain to it …etc and then signed by the President, chairman of trustees, etc. I felt like I earned that one. And I did.

The PhD program I went through was challenging, work and much research and study. But was rewarding as the dissertation will soon become a published book.

I have another one though that says practically the same thing it's from Campbellsville College, now University and it says the degree of Doctor of Divinity with all it honors, rights, privileges and responsibilities thereto appertaining and then signed by College officials.

When I received the one from Campbellsville I have to admit I was humbled, and felt incredibly unworthy. While I worked hard and toiled for the other degrees I have this one was given the year I was President of the Kentucky Baptist Convention and is an honorary degree.

There is a great graduation day coming. The Lord Jesus will be handing out the diplomas. And when we stand before the Lord Jesus and hear our name called and we are recipients of a diploma that has our name on it and says, 'with all the honors, rights, privileges and responsibilities thereto appertaining." I honestly don't think you or I will stand in the presence of Christ and feel worthy or deserving.

There are those blessings of life that we feel like we earned. But most of the time we are like Abraham who clearly is a story of God's grace. There are those gifts and blessings that God gives to us. These are eternal life, forgiveness of our sins and all the blessings that come with simply trusting and obeying God day by day.

Today we praise the name of God. You trusted him to bring you to this point of graduation. You obeyed him by yielding to His call upon your life. You followed God's leading by training and preparing for greater service. Today you are receiving your degree! Congratulations to you! Well done good and faithful servant! God now has much greater opportunities ahead for you! To God be the glory!